HERITAGE STUDIES 1

Third Edition

bju press®

Greenville, South Carolina

Note

The fact that materials produced by other publishers may be referred to in this volume does not constitute an endorsement of the content or theological position of materials produced by such publishers. Any references and ancillary materials are listed as an aid to the student or the teacher and in an attempt to maintain the accepted academic standards of the publishing industry.

Heritage Studies 1
Third Edition

Authors
Eileen Berry
Gina Bradstreet
Ann Larson
L. Michelle Rosier

Bible Integration
Bryan Smith

Consultants
Dottie Buckley
Jim Davis
Katie Klipp
Dennis Peterson

Project Editor
Carolyn Cooper

Designer
Michael Asire

Cover Design
Elly Kalagayan

Cover Illustration
Ben Schipper

Cover Photography
Craig Oesterling

Page Layout
Bonnijean Marley

Project Managers
Amy Johnson
Faith Larson

Permissions
Sylvia Gass
Ashley Hobbs
Kristin Villalba

Illustration Coordinator
Del Thompson

Illustrators
Paula Cheadle
Preston Gravely
Dave Schuppert
Lynda Slattery
Courtney Godbey Wise

Photograph credits start on page 198.

Unless otherwise specified, all poems and rhymes are original works by BJU Press authors.

Produced in cooperation with the Bob Jones University School of Education and Bob Jones Academy.

© 2013 BJU Press
Greenville, South Carolina 29614
First Edition © 1979 BJU Press
Second Edition © 1996 BJU Press

ISBN 978-1-60682-208-1

15 14 13 12 11 10 9 8 7 6 5 4 3 2 1

Contents

Chapter

1: God's World   6

2: Your Family   22

3: Your Community   34

4: Your State   50

5: Your Country   66

6: Your Country's Capital   80

7: Native Americans   96

8: Christopher Columbus   110

9: Jamestown   124

10: Plymouth   144

11: Today and Long Ago   162

Resource Treasury   172

Geogloss   174

Atlas   176

Picture Glossary   180

Index   191

What is Heritage Studies?

The BJU Press Heritage Studies materials are a presentation of social studies that integrates civics, culture, economics, geography, and history. Beginning with the framework of God's redemptive plan, *Heritage Studies 1* includes an age-appropriate study of civics and government and then covers United States history from Native Americans to the Plymouth Colony, all from a Christian worldview. The final chapter contrasts the past and the present, noting changes that have taken place in the way we live. Poems, eye-catching artwork, maps, graphs, photos, quick-check questions, and an extended hands-on activity enhance learning.

To Learn

To learn is to go sailing
To a new and distant shore.
To learn is to meet people
I have never met before.

Geography

History

To learn is to find treasure
In a place I'd never look.
To learn is to grow wiser
As I travel through my book.

Economics

Culture

Citizenship

Exploring Our Book

Learn new things.

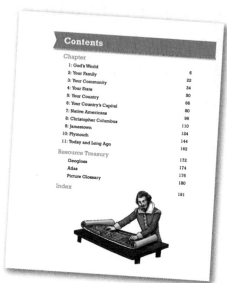

Contents

Chapter

1: God's World
2: Your Family 6
3: Your Community 22
4: Your State 34
5: Your Country 50
6: Your Country's Capital 66
7: Native Americans 80
8: Christopher Columbus 96
9: Jamestown 110
10: Plymouth 124
11: Today and Long Ago 144
.... 162

Resource Treasury

Geogloss 172
Atlas 174
Picture Glossary 176
.... 180
Index 191

Enjoy pictures.

My God Knows

Big, wide world—
Land and sea, moon and stars;
I'm just one small speck
In this big, wide world of ours.

But my great, good God,
Who made everything I see,
Knows me inside out,
And He loves and cares for me.

★

Vocabulary

- continent
- directions
- globe
- map
- ocean
- Savior

God's World 1

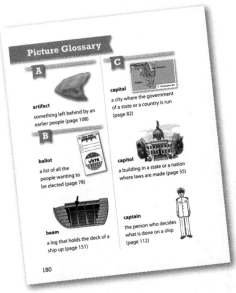

Picture Glossary

A

artifact
something left behind by an earlier people (page 108)

B

ballot
a list of all the people wanting to be elected (page 78)

beam
a log that holds the deck of a ship up (page 151)

C

capital
a city where the government of a state or a country is run (page 82)

capitol
a building in a state or a nation where laws are made (page 55)

captain
the person who decides what is done on a ship (page 112)

180

Read new words.

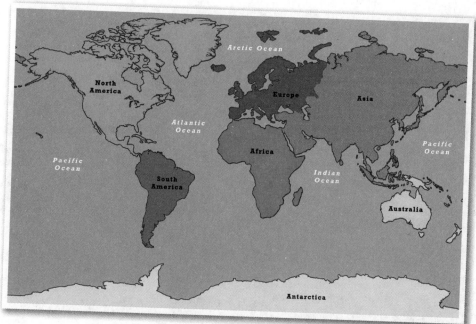

Study a map.

My God Knows

Big, wide world—
Land and sea, moon and stars;
I'm just one small speck
In this big, wide world of ours.

But my great, good God,
Who made everything I see,
Knows me inside out,
And He loves and cares for me.

★

Vocabulary

- continent
- directions
- globe
- map
- ocean
- Savior

God's World

God Made the World

In the beginning God made the world.
God made it out of nothing.
He just spoke.
Then the world was there.

God made everything in the world.
He made light.
He made the sky.
He made the land and the sea.
He made tiny flowers and tall trees.
He made the sun, the moon, and the stars.

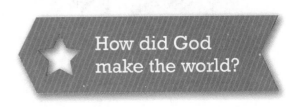

How did God make the world?

God Made Animals

God made animals.
He made shiny fish and bright birds.
He made big cats.
He made quick rabbits.
He made shy deer.
He made little bugs.

God Made People

God made people too.
God made a man.
The man was Adam.
God made a woman.
The woman was Eve.
God told them to have children.
He told them to care for His world.

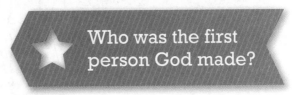

Who was the first person God made?

Sin and a Savior

God's world was perfect.
It had nothing bad in it.
God gave Adam and Eve one rule.
They could not eat from one tree.
Adam and Eve broke the rule.
They sinned.
Then God's world was no longer perfect.

But God had a plan.
He would send a **Savior** one day.
This Savior would be perfect.
He would save people from their sin.

Who did God
plan to send?

People in the World

God wanted people to live in every part
of the world.
Adam and Eve had children.
Their children had children.
People moved to many different places.
Now people live all over the world.

The World

God's world has water and land.
Look at the **map**.
A map is a drawing that shows
where places are.
The blue color shows water.
The green color shows land.
People live in almost all the green places.

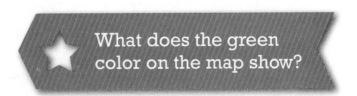

What does the green
color on the map show?

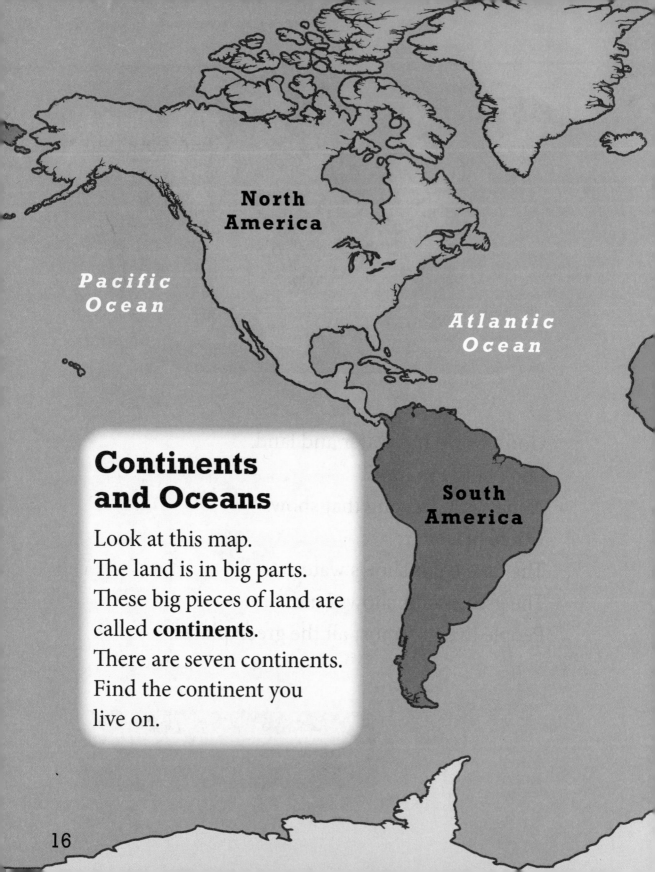

North America

Pacific Ocean

Atlantic Ocean

Continents and Oceans

Look at this map.
The land is in big parts.
These big pieces of land are
called **continents**.
There are seven continents.
Find the continent you
live on.

South America

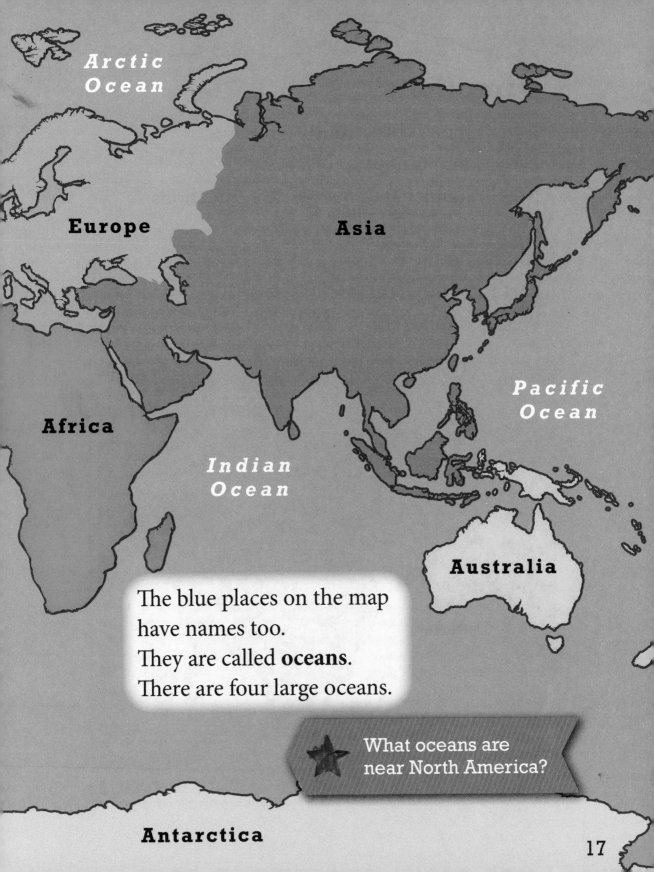

Arctic
Ocean

Europe

Asia

Pacific
Ocean

Africa

Indian
Ocean

Australia

The blue places on the map
have names too.
They are called **oceans**.
There are four large oceans.

What oceans are
near North America?

Antarctica

Directions

A map shows **directions**.

Directions point us to places.

North, south, east, and west are directions.

On this map north is at the top.

South is at the bottom.

East is on the right.

West is on the left.

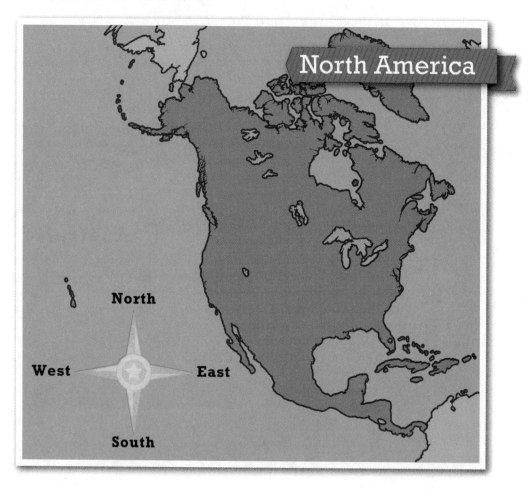

The Globe

This is a **globe**.
A globe shows the shape
of the world.
A globe is shaped like a ball.
You can turn a globe to see
different places.
You can find the seven
continents and the four
oceans.

The earth looks like this
from space.

Can you find your
continent on a globe?

Activity

Different Places, Different Ways

The people in the world are not all alike.
Not all people do things the same way.
People in different places have different ways.

Some people eat food like this.

Some people dress like this.

Some people live in homes like this.

God loves people in every part of the world.

What is one thing people do in different ways?

20

Famous People

Hudson Taylor

Hudson Taylor lived in Europe.
God led him to another
continent.
God led him to go to China
in Asia.
Hudson Taylor told people
in China about the Savior,
Jesus Christ.

But Chinese people had different ways.
So Hudson Taylor changed his ways.
He dressed like the people of China.
He ate their food.
Many people in China trusted Jesus.

Together

My mother and my father
Care for me so lovingly,
And together we're the family
God created us to be.

---★---

Vocabulary

- family
- needs
- role
- rules
- wants

Your Family

The First Family

Adam and Eve began the first **family**.

God made Adam first.

Adam and Eve had two sons.

They named their sons Cain and Abel.

They were the first family.

Their family had a father, a mother, and children.

God made Eve to help Adam.

Eve cooked the food.

Adam plowed the land.

Cain planted a garden.

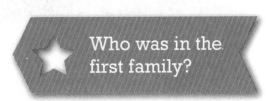

Abel took care of the sheep.

Who was in the first family?

25

Families

God planned for you to live in a family.
He wants you to have a father and a mother.
Each family member has a **role**.
A role is the special part each person plays
in a family.
Fathers and mothers care for their children.
Everyone in a family works together.

This dad is teaching his little girl how to fish.

This is the first family.

This is a family today.

God had a plan.

He wanted families in every part of the earth.

Families can be found everywhere.

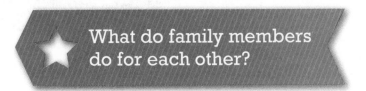

What do family members
do for each other?

Families Work and Play

Families help each other.
They also have fun together.
Some people in a family work in the home.
Some people work away from home.

Working together is fun.

This family likes to play games inside.

This family likes to play outside.

What do families do?

Family Rules

Families have **rules**.

God gives rules to families.

The Bible says to obey your mom and dad.

Rules let you know what you must do.

Rules let you know what you should not do.

Following rules protects you.

Rules help everyone in a family get along.

Families Love God

The Bible teaches you about God.
It teaches you to love and obey
your mom and dad.

This family reads the Bible.

This family goes to church.

How do rules help you?

Needs and Wants

Everyone has needs.

Needs are things a family must have to live.
A family needs things like food, clothes, and shelter.

This mom has cooked a meal for her family.

Each person in a family needs love and care.
People work to get money.
Families use money to buy things they need.

Families also buy some things they want.

Wants are things people would like to have.

But people cannot have all they want.

They must make choices about how to spend their money.

Families give money to God's work.

Be thankful for your family.

This dad builds houses.

What things do all people need?

Activity

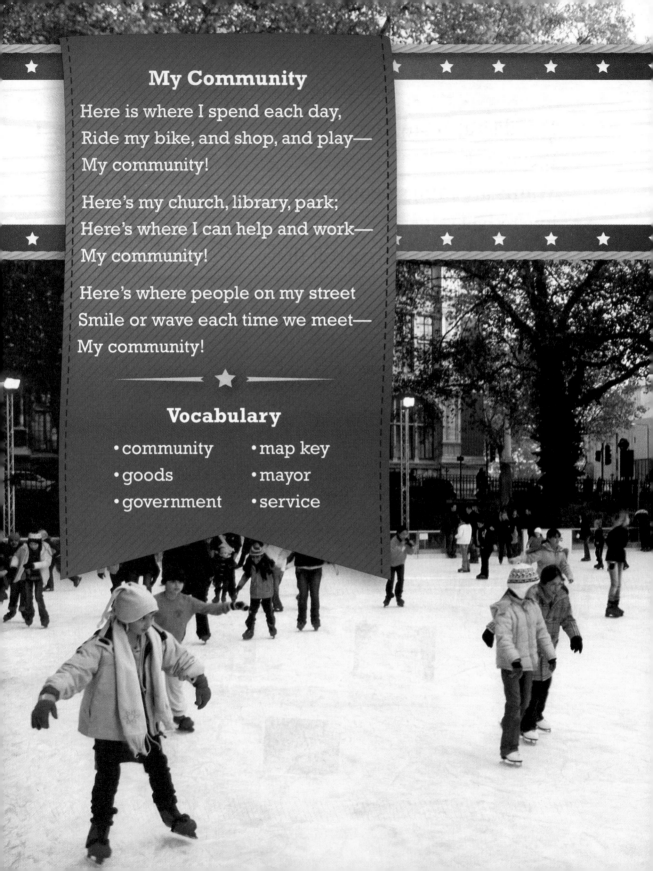

My Community

Here is where I spend each day,
Ride my bike, and shop, and play—
My community!

Here's my church, library, park;
Here's where I can help and work—
My community!

Here's where people on my street
Smile or wave each time we meet—
My community!

Vocabulary

- community
- goods
- government
- map key
- mayor
- service

Your Community

Your Community

Your family lives in a **community**.
People that live near your family make
a community.
People working near where your family lives
are a part of your community.
People living or working together make
a community.

Many people in a community work.
Farmers grow food. Foods are **goods**.
Goods are things people make, grow, or sell.
Some people make goods we need.
Other people sell goods we use.

What makes a community?

Your Community Helpers

A doctor helps people stay well.

A police officer helps to keep you safe.

A pastor serves the community too.

A **service** is something that helps people.

Community helpers serve people.

This teacher uses hand signs to teach.

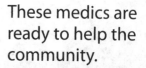

A letter carrier delivers the mail.

These medics are ready to help the community.

God wants you to serve people
in a special way.
You can offer to help people
in your community.
The Bible says to serve one another
with love.

Galatians 5:13

By love serve one another.

The man tells children about Jesus.

A family serves people with no home.

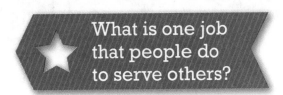

What is one job
that people do
to serve others?

Your Community Places

People work in many different places
in your community.
A farmer may sell apples from his truck.
The lady next door may cut hair in a shop.
Also, people visit many different places
in your community.
You may like to eat a snack at the bakery.
You may visit a park or the library.

This lady works at a flower shop in her community.

A family works at the church.

Families play at the park.

A boy learns at the museum.

 What place in your community do you like to visit?

41

Helping in Your Community

Your family is part of a community.
You are part of a community.
God wants you to help other people
in your community.
God wants you to take care of the place
where you live.
God's plan is that you care for others
and for the community.

You can help keep the lake and land clean.

You can help people who live near you.

Community Paper Drive

Fire Station	📄	📄	📄	
Todd's Store	📄	📄	📄	📄
Bible Church	📄	📄	📄	

Many communities recycle paper.

How can you help your community?

Your Community Leaders

Many communities near each other make a city.

A city has leaders.

The leader of a city is a **mayor**.

The mayor helps make laws.

He works to make the community better.

The mayor works for the community.

A community helper clears the street.

A city worker keeps the community safe.

All the city workers form the city **government**. The government workers serve the people of the community. These workers care for the people. They make the city a better place to live.

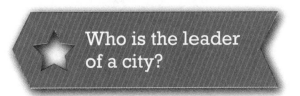

Who is the leader of a city?

A Community Long Ago

Long ago Ben Franklin lived in the city
of Philadelphia.

Mr. Franklin worked to make his city better.

He enjoyed serving the people.

Mr. Franklin started the first library.

He began a fire department in his city.

Ben Franklin started the first post office.

He also set up a hospital to help the sick.

Benjamin Franklin

Mr. Franklin liked to read.

Then and Now

Comparing Philadelphia

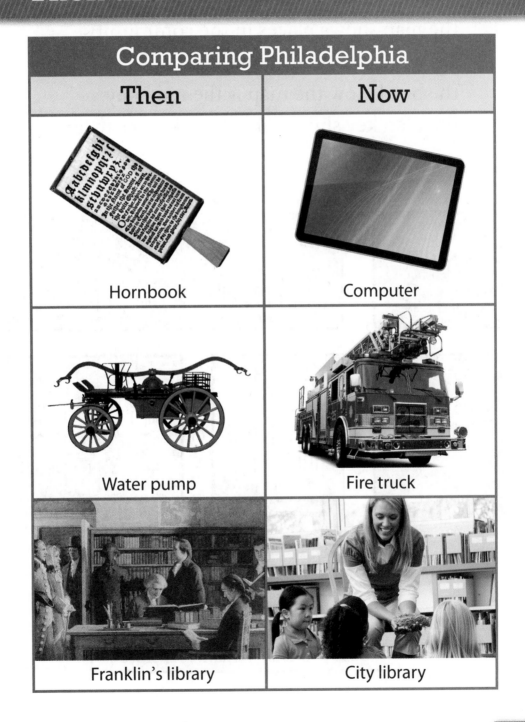

Then	Now
Hornbook	Computer
Water pump	Fire truck
Franklin's library	City library

Finding Your Community

The map shows places in the community.
It is a drawing that shows where places are.
The box below the map is the **map key**.
The map key shows what the pictures mean.

Community Map

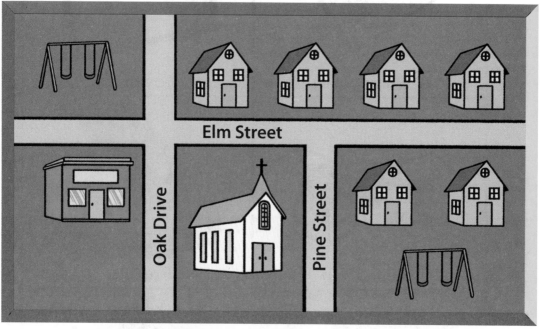

Families living and working together make
a community.

Communities near each other form a city.

The mayor is the leader of the city.

Community leaders work for the government.

People working together make a community
a good place to live.

Activity

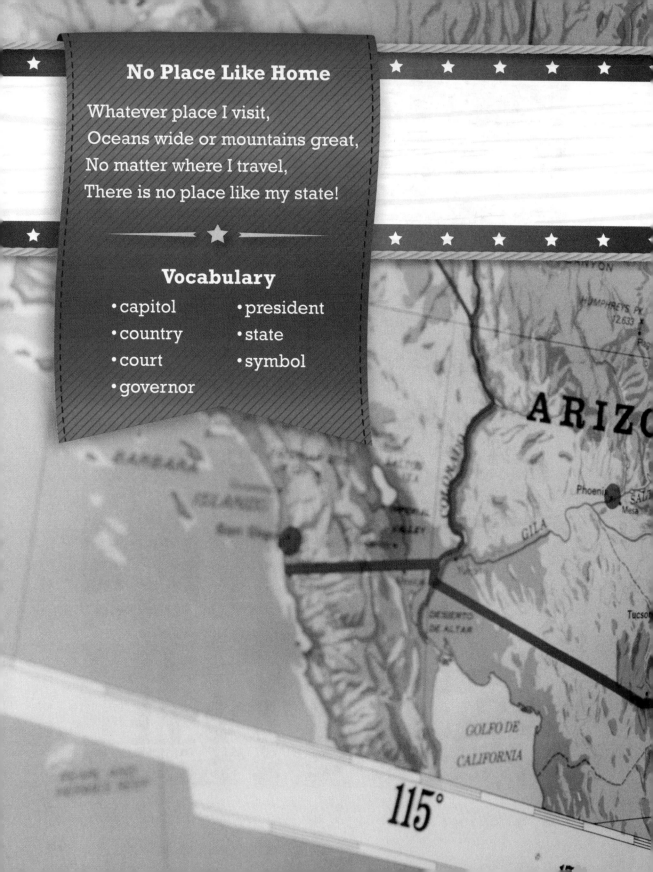

No Place Like Home

Whatever place I visit,
Oceans wide or mountains great,
No matter where I travel,
There is no place like my state!

★

Vocabulary

- capitol
- country
- court
- governor
- president
- state
- symbol

Your State

4

You Live in a State

Your community is a part of a **state**.

A state is a part of a **country**.

A country is a land with its own people and laws.

Our country is the United States of America.

There are fifty states in the United States.

You live in one of these states.

A state sign welcomes you to a state.

Your state has a flag.
It has a special bird.
It has a special flower.
It has its own shape.
No other state is quite like yours.

Maryland
state flower

Indiana state bird

Florida state flag

What state do
you live in?

Your State Has Leaders

People in a state choose their government leaders.

Your state has a **governor**.

The governor leads your state.

He works with the people who make laws.

God wants you to pray for your leaders (1 Timothy 2:1–2).

Your state has a **capitol** building.

Laws are made at the capitol.

Your state also has **courts**.

Judges in courts use laws to settle problems.

They decide what is just and right.

Who leads a state?

55

States Have Famous People

Famous people lived in some states.

This state was home to a famous man.

His name was George Washington Carver.

Dr. Carver was born a slave.

He learned to read, write, draw, and farm.

Dr. Carver found many ways to use plants.

He taught farmers to use plants wisely.

Alabama

This state was home to a famous woman.
Her name was Clara Barton.
Miss Barton was a brave nurse.
She cared for men who had been hurt
in battles.
She helped families find missing men.
She started the American Red Cross.
The Red Cross still cares for people today.

Maryland

How did Dr. Carver and
Miss Barton help people?

States Have Famous Places

This state has a famous place.

The place is called Mount Rushmore.

You can see four faces in the rock.

They are faces of United States **presidents**.

A president is a leader of our country.

Mount Rushmore makes us think of great men.

These men helped make our country great.

South Dakota

Arizona

This state has a famous place too.
The place is called the Grand Canyon.
Many people go to see the tall cliffs
and the river.
The Grand Canyon is made of rock.
The Grand Canyon makes us think
of our great God.

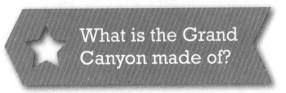
What is the Grand Canyon made of?

This state also has a famous place.
The place is called the Great Lakes.
There are five deep lakes around this state.
People fish and sail on the lakes.
The land is in two parts.
Look at your right hand.
The lower part of the state looks
like your hand.

Michigan

California

This state has a famous place.
It is a huge bridge.
The Golden Gate Bridge is very long.
Cars drive across a bay on the bridge.

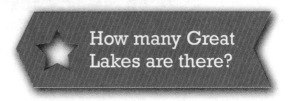

How many Great
Lakes are there?

States Have Famous Things

Some states have famous things.

This state has a famous bell.

The Liberty Bell was made long ago.

The bell was rung in 1776.

The Liberty Bell is a **symbol** of freedom.

A symbol stands for something else.

Pennsylvania

This state also has a famous symbol.
It is called the Statue of Liberty.
The statue is of a tall lady.
She wears a crown.
She holds a torch up to the sky.
People see the statue and remember
that our country is free.

New York

What does the bell
make us think of?

Alaska

This state is cold and snowy.
This state has a famous race.
It is a special dog sled race.
Dogs pull sleds many miles in the snow.
The fastest dogs win.

Every state has something important about it.
Every state is special.

What is special
about your state?

Activity

Kansas

Fireworks

Kaboom! Crackle-pop!
Big bursts of bright light—
Glowing sky-spiders
Trailing down through the night.

Kaboom! Sizzle-bang!
What a show up above!
A grand celebration
For the land that we love.

Vocabulary

- ballot
- citizen
- election
- motto
- pledge
- right
- vote

Your Country

The United States of America

Your country is called the United States of America.

A country is a land with its own people and laws.

There are fifty states in the United States.

The United States is called the Land of the Free.

Here is the United States on a globe.

Canada is the country north
of the United States.
Mexico is the country south
of the United States.

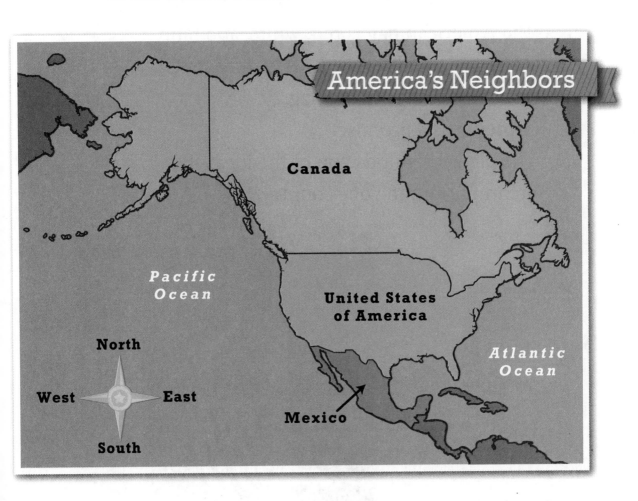

America's Neighbors

Canada

Pacific
Ocean

United States
of America

Atlantic
Ocean

North

West   East

South

Mexico

What is a country?

Your Country's Flag

The American flag is a symbol of the
United States of America.
Symbols stand for things that are important.
The American flag is red, white, and blue.
Each star stands for one of the fifty states.
You say a pledge to the flag.
A **pledge** is a promise.
The pledge reminds you of the ideas that
are important to your country.

Many Americans fly
a flag on Flag Day.

The Pledge

I pledge allegiance to the flag
of the United States of America,
and to the republic for which
it stands,
one nation under God,
indivisible,
with liberty and justice for all.

What is a pledge?

Symbols of Your Country

The United States has many other symbols.
Your country has a **motto**.
A motto is an important saying.
"In God we trust" is the motto
of the United States.

The motto is printed on
your country's money.

The bald eagle is a symbol
of your country.
An eagle is strong and free.

"The Star-Spangled Banner" is your
country's song.
It is sung before sports games and
at concerts.
People should stand when they hear
"The Star-Spangled Banner."
They also put their hand over their heart.
Men and boys take off their hats.

"The Star-Spangled Banner"

What is a motto?

America the Beautiful

O beautiful for spacious skies,
For amber waves of grain,

For purple mountain majesties
Above the fruited plain!

America! America!
God shed His grace on thee,
And crown thy good with brotherhood
From sea to shining sea!

Do you live near an ocean or a mountain?

Your Country's Leaders

The president is the leader of your country.
He lives with his family in the White House.
Lawmakers make new laws.
Laws help keep the country safe.
A judge decides if people are following the laws.
The Constitution is a set of laws.
The president, lawmakers, and judges must
follow the Constitution.

The Constitution of
the United States
of America

Citizens

A **citizen** is a member of a country.
You are a citizen of the United States
of America if you are born here.
A person from another country can also
become a citizen of the United States.
Citizens of a country have rights.
A **right** is something you are free to do.
Citizens also have a duty to their country.
Good citizens follow the laws of their country.
Laws make a country a better place to live.

New citizens of
the United States

★ What is a citizen?

Elections

An **election** is held to choose new leaders.
Citizens choose or **vote** for their leaders.
They need to choose wisely.

Step 1: People give speeches.
They put their signs here and there.
They want people to vote for them.

Step 2: Citizens use a **ballot** to vote.
The ballot is a list of all the people
who want to be elected.

Step 3: All the votes are counted.

This sign is in a yard.

Step 4: The people with the most votes become the new leaders.

The United States of America is the country God has given you to live in.

God wants you to be a good citizen of your country.

Voting machines make it faster to vote.

How are new leaders chosen?

Activity

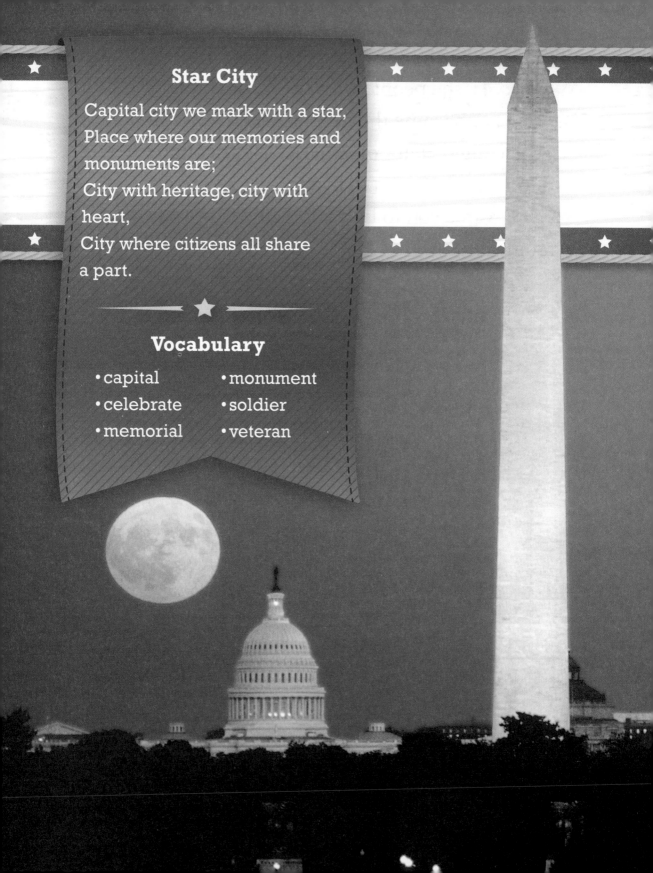

Star City

Capital city we mark with a star,
Place where our memories and monuments are;
City with heritage, city with heart,
City where citizens all share a part.

★

Vocabulary

- capital
- celebrate
- memorial
- monument
- soldier
- veteran

Your Country's Capital

6

Washington, DC

The **capital** of the United States of America
is Washington, DC.
It is a very important city in America.
The United States government is run here.
Many government leaders work here.
You can visit many special buildings
in the capital city.

The Capitol Building

The United States Capitol Building
is in Washington, DC.
The Capitol is the building
where lawmakers work.
Lawmakers use the Constitution
to make laws for the country.

United States Capitol

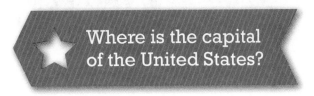

Where is the capital
of the United States?

The White House

The president's house is in Washington, DC.
It is called the White House.
The president and his family live there.
People from all over the world visit
the White House.
You can visit it too.

Many people visit the White House.

Children in the White House

The president's children have favorite foods.
Sasha Obama likes ice cream.
The president's children can have a pet.
Young Ted Roosevelt had a bird named Eli.
Children can play hide-and-seek in the 132
rooms of the White House.
Little John Kennedy liked to hide under the
desk in the president's office.

Sasha Obama

Ted Roosevelt Jr.

John Kennedy Jr.

⭐ Where does the president live?

The Washington Monument

A **monument** is something built that stands for a person in the past.

The Washington Monument is the tallest monument in Washington, DC.

It is made from stone.

There are fifty American flags around the bottom of the monument.

The Washington Monument reminds us of a great man, George Washington.

What is the tallest monument in Washington, DC?

George Washington

The American people loved George Washington.

It is said that he was "first in war, first in peace, and first in the hearts of his countrymen."

God gave us a wise man to be the first president of the United States.

America **celebrates** his birthday in February on Presidents' Day.

World War II Memorial

A **memorial** helps you remember people or times from the past.

The World War II Memorial reminds you of the many **soldiers** who served in that war. These soldiers loved America and helped to keep their country safe.

Veterans Day

On November 11, America celebrates
Veterans Day.
A **veteran** is someone who has served
our country in the armed forces.
America honors war veterans with parades
on this special day.

A veteran from World War II

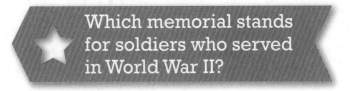

Which memorial stands
for soldiers who served
in World War II?

Lincoln Memorial

The Lincoln Memorial honors President
Abraham Lincoln.
The stone building is very large.
The huge statue of President Lincoln is inside.
He is sitting in a big chair.
He looks like he is thinking.
You feel small when you look at the giant
statue of Mr. Lincoln.

Abraham Lincoln

Abraham Lincoln was the sixteenth
president of the United States.
He grew up in a log cabin.
He loved to read.
People trusted Mr. Lincoln because
he was honest.
He is called Honest Abe.

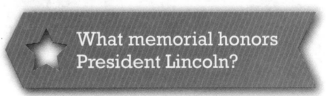

What memorial honors
President Lincoln?

Independence Day Parade

A parade takes place in Washington, DC, on July 4. The parade celebrates America's freedom from England.

On July 4, 1776, a paper was signed saying that America was free from England. Our country celebrates this freedom with parades and fireworks.

How do you celebrate the Fourth of July?

Activity

Landmarks in Washington, DC

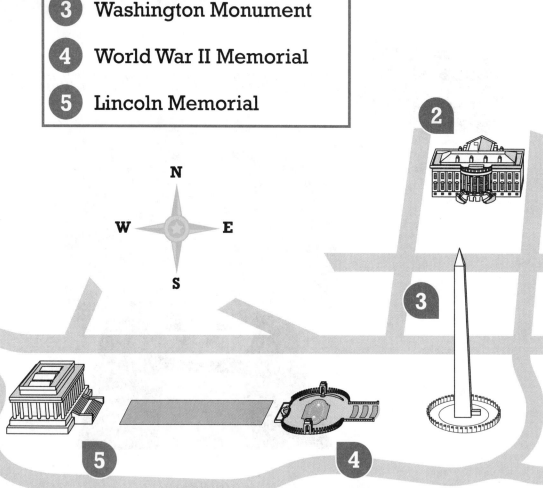

Map Key

1 Capitol

2 White House

3 Washington Monument

4 World War II Memorial

5 Lincoln Memorial

N
W E
S

Star City

Eileen M. Berry

Capital city we mark with a star,
Place where our memories and monuments are;
Bustling with tourists and traffic and trains,
Cherry trees blooming in parks and on lanes.

City with heritage, city with heart,
City where citizens all share a part.
See all the flags—for our freedom they stand!
God by His grace has protected our land.

Pennsylvania Avenue

Constitution Avenue

1

Independence Avenue

Song of Our Homeland

Woodland and seashore,
Desert dune,
Home to our people
Many a moon.

Grassland and hillside
Long we roamed,
Here in the land
You now call home.

Vocabulary

- artifact
- culture
- native
- tepee
- totem pole
- tribe

Native Americans

7

The First Americans

People first came to live in North America long ago.
After the Flood, Noah's children had children.
Their children also had children.
There were more and more people in the world.
People scattered all around the world as God had told them to do.
Some people went to North America.

The first Americans came from far away.

We call these first Americans and their children Indians or Native Americans. A **native** is a person born in a certain place. Native Americans lived in different groups. The groups lived in all different parts of North America.

Native Americans lived and worked in groups.

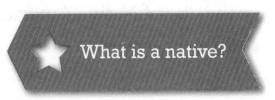

What is a native?

Native American Groups

Some groups lived in the forests.
Some groups lived on the flat, grassy plains.
Some groups lived on the coasts.
Some groups lived in the dry, sandy deserts.
These groups were called **tribes**.
Each tribe of Native Americans had its own
culture, or way of life.

Most Native Americans did not worship
the true God.
They worshiped many spirits instead.
They thought these spirits lived in trees, rivers,
wind, and rain.
These beliefs were a large part of their culture.
Many of the things they did were their way
of trying to please the spirits.

What were
Native American
groups called?

People of the Plains

Some Native Americans lived on the grassy
plains in the middle of North America.
One of these tribes was the Kiowa.
The Kiowa men were hunters.
They hunted the buffalo that grazed
on the plains.
The Kiowa people ate buffalo meat.
They moved often, following the buffalo herds.

Kiowa people made clothes and shoes from buffalo skins.

Kiowa women cared for children, cooked, and kept the homes.
Kiowa homes needed to be easy to move.
Each Kiowa family set up wooden poles in a cone shape.
They covered the poles with buffalo hides.
The hides kept out the cold and the rain.
The Kiowa painted animals and other pictures on the hides.
These homes were called **tepees**.

Tepee poles and hides were easy to move.

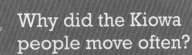

Why did the Kiowa people move often?

People of the Southwest

Many Native Americans of the Southwest were farmers.

They lived in the hot desert where little rain fell.

But they knew how to grow corn, beans, and squash for food.

They also wove cloth and formed pots out of clay.

Many used dry grass and plants to make baskets.

Some Southwest people built homes high in the cliffs.
Their homes can still be seen today.
The Hopi tribe made homes of mud and bricks.
Many of their homes had two or three floors.
The Hopi climbed ladders to go from floor to floor.
On hot nights, they slept on the rooftops under the stars.

Hopi homes

Cliff homes

What did the Hopi people grow for food?

People of the Northwest Coast

The Native Americans who lived along the Northwest Coast were fishermen. They built sturdy canoes from the trunks of trees. They took their canoes out on the sea. They hunted fish, seals, and whales in the deep waters.

Northwest Coast Indians ate fish and whale meat.

One tribe, the Tlingit, lived on the coast of what is now Alaska. Their homes needed to last through storms. They built strong wooden homes. They placed tall poles around the sides of their houses. These **totem poles** were carved with pictures of people and animals.

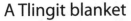

Totem pole

A Tlingit blanket

What did the Tlingit people place around their homes?

Activity

Native American Artifacts

Today most Native Americans live the way we do.

Most do not build tepees or make shoes from animal skins.

But some Native Americans from long ago left things behind.

We call these things **artifacts**.

Most artifacts were made from things the Native Americans found in God's world.

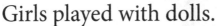

Girls played with dolls.
Both men and women wore beads.
Bone tools were used for building
and farming.
Stone arrows were used for hunting.
Stone balls were used in games.
Artifacts help us remember how
the first Americans lived.

How are these artifacts like things we use today?

Dreams and Plans

When Christopher was just a boy,
The harbor was his greatest joy.
He watched the big ships come
    and go;
But little did the young boy know
What God had planned for him
    one day:
To find a new world far away.

Vocabulary

- captain
- explore
- sailor
- voyage

Christopher Columbus

8

Christopher Columbus

Christopher Columbus lived in a large city near the sea.

He dreamed of being the **captain** of a ship someday.

A captain decides what is done on a ship.

When he grew up, Columbus sailed to many places.

He read many books.

He learned how to draw maps.

People wanted to find a faster way to reach Asia
by ship.
They wanted the gold and spices found there.
Columbus talked with many **sailors**.
Sailors do the work on ships.
Some of the sailors had seen land in the west
that had not been explored.
To **explore** means to find out about a new place.

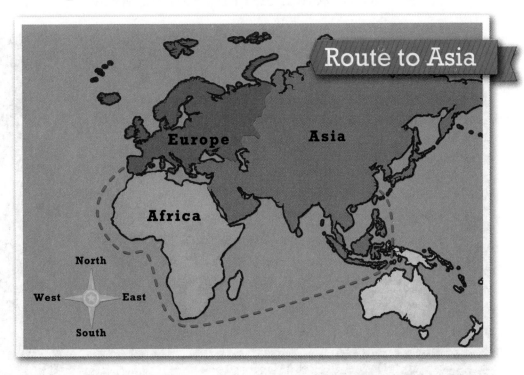

Route to Asia

Europe

Asia

Africa

North

West — East

South

Ships sailed around
Africa to get to Asia.

Who does the
work on ships?

The First Maps

When Columbus lived, people did not know
how large the earth really is.
Many people thought it was only a little
smaller than it really is.
Columbus thought it was much smaller.
Columbus thought there might be a shorter,
faster way to reach Asia by sailing west.

The earth is very large.

The first maps were not like those used today. They showed only the land men had explored. People did not know that two continents lay between them and Asia.

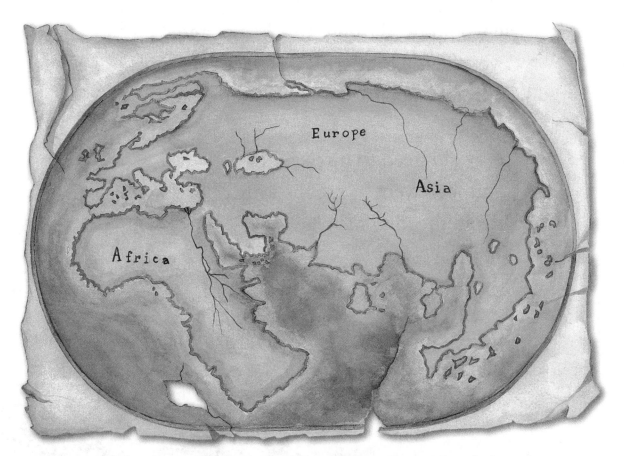

The first maps did not have North America or South America.

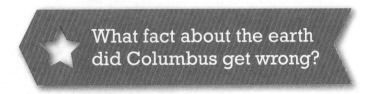
What fact about the earth did Columbus get wrong?

A Visit to the King and Queen

Columbus began to plan a trip to Asia.
He thought he could get to Asia faster
by sailing west.
He would need things for the **voyage**.
A voyage is a long trip to a place far away.
Columbus needed money for ships and
supplies.
He would need to hire sailors.
Columbus went to see the king of Portugal.
He told the king his plan.

Columbus needed money for his voyage.

Columbus asked the king for money.
He said he would bring back gold and spices from Asia.
The king of Portugal did not want to help Columbus.
He thought Columbus was wrong about the size of the earth.
Columbus then went to see King Ferdinand and Queen Isabella of Spain.

Columbus asked the king and queen for help.

Columbus explained his plan to the king and queen.

They thought about what Columbus said. Years later they decided to help him. Columbus soon had three ships to use for his voyage.

He packed enough food to last a year. He hired sailors to help on the ships. His dream to be a captain had come true.

The *Niña*, the *Pinta*, and the *Santa María*

How many ships did Columbus use for his voyage?

A Long Voyage

The ships' sails were raised, and the voyage began.
The days were long and hard.
Weeks went by, but Columbus did not find land.
Some of the sailors began to grumble.
They did not want to keep going.

Some of the sailors wanted to turn back.

Columbus did not want to end the voyage yet.
He decided to turn back if they did not see
land in three days.
The next day one of the men spotted land.
The sun was not up yet.
Most of the sailors were still sleeping.
"Land!" a sailor yelled. "Land!"

Columbus was happy to find land.

Columbus did not reach Asia by sailing west.
Though Columbus did not know where he
landed, God did.
Columbus did not know he had found new
lands to explore.
God used the voyage to change the world.

Columbus called the people he found Indians,
and he claimed the land for Spain.

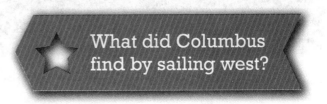

What did Columbus
find by sailing west?

Today and Long Ago

Ships

Long ago ships were made from wood.
The wood was cut and shaped by hand.
The ship was rolled to the water on a cart.

Boards were used to make the ship.

Today most ships are made from steel.

Columbus Day

Columbus Day is celebrated on the second Monday of October.
It is a day to remember Christopher Columbus and the land he found.
It is a day to remember what God did long ago.

Christopher Columbus

Activity

To a Wild New Shore

Over the sea
The English came,
To a wild new shore
And a land untamed.

The men worked hard,
And the rough years passed;
By the grace of God
Jamestown would last.

★

Vocabulary

- chief
- fort
- resource
- servant
- settlement

Jamestown

Sailing Across the Ocean

Many years had passed since Christopher Columbus had landed in the New World. English men heard about the New World too. They wanted some of the land called America. These men hoped to find gold and riches there.

Men made maps showing the way to the New World.

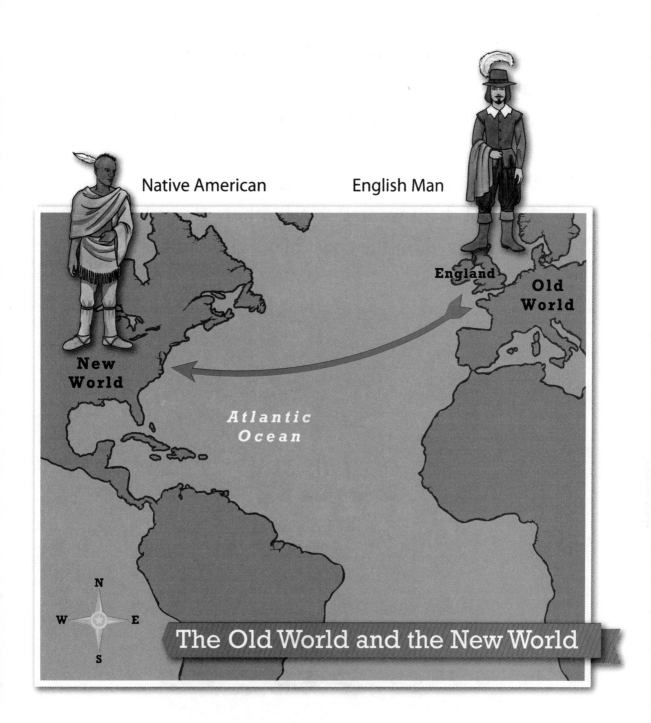

Native American

English Man

England

Old World

New World

Atlantic Ocean

N W E S

The Old World and the New World

Three ships left England for the part of America called Virginia.

Many rich men and some workers and boys sailed in the ships.

Most of them wanted riches.

A few of them wanted to tell others about Jesus.

They arrived on the coast of Virginia in May of 1607.

The ships were named the *Discovery*, the *Susan Constant*, and the *Godspeed*.

The ships sailed up a river.
The men named it the James River
after their king, King James.
They called the place where they landed
Jamestown.

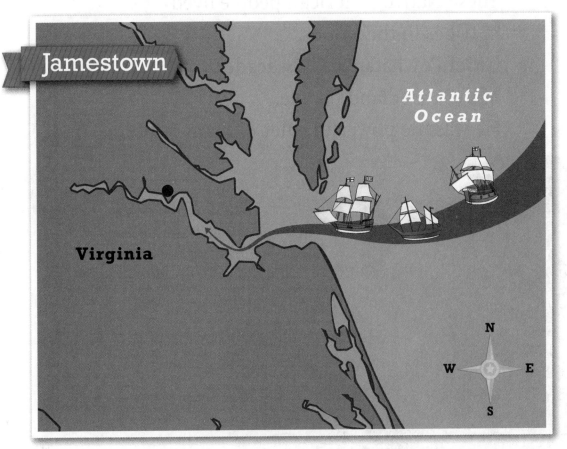

The dot (●) shows where Jamestown is.

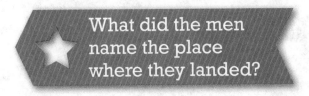

What did the men name the place where they landed?

Meeting the Woodland People

When English ships sailed up the river,
the Woodland people were watching.
These Native American people lived
in tribes in the woods.
Chief Powhatan was the leader
of the Woodland people.
He was the powerful ruler of many tribes.

A Woodland man watched the ships sail up the river.

Strangers had come to their land.
Some tribes did not want the English to live
on their land.
Other tribes were friendly to the English men.
The chief was not sure what to think
of these strangers.
But he let the English people stay.
The English men had guns, copper, and beads.
Chief Powhatan wanted these things.

Powhatan was the chief of many Woodland tribes.

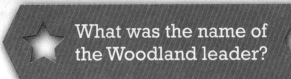

What was the name of the Woodland leader?

Starting a Settlement

The leaders of Jamestown made a plan.
They would build a **fort**.
The fort would keep them safe.
The men cut the trees to clear the land.
Trees were used for the walls of the fort.
The fort was built in the shape of a triangle.
Houses, buildings, and a church were built inside the fort walls.
Jamestown Fort became the first English **settlement**.
A settlement is a group of people living in a new place.

This ax head was found in diggings at Jamestown.

Courtesy Preservation Virginia

The ax was used to chop trees for the fort.

George Percy 1607

"The fifteenth of June we had built and finished our Fort, which was triangle wise."

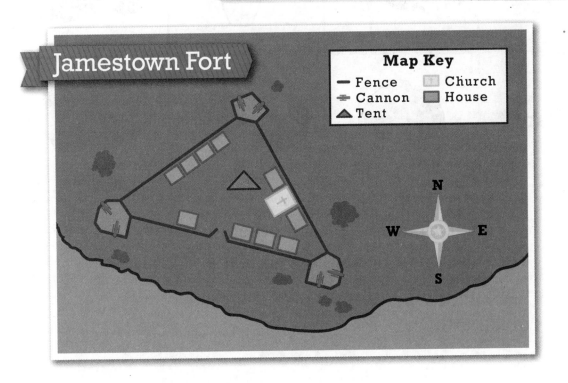

Jamestown Fort

Map Key
- Fence
- Cannon
- Tent
- Church
- House

N
W — E
S

Living in a Settlement

Much work needed to be done to make
the fort a good place to live.
Everyone was needed to plant crops
and hunt for food.
But the rich men did not want to work.
They looked for gold but did not find it.

	Jamestown Needs and Wants		
Needs	food	water	fort
Wants	gold	gems	furs

The men argued with each other.
The settlement needed a wise leader.
Captain John Smith became the leader
of Jamestown.

If any would not work,
neither should he eat.

Captain Smith used a truth from God's Word
to get the men to work.
If a man did not work, he could not eat.
All the men soon learned to work.
It was a hard job planting seeds in the dirt.
The crops did not grow well.
More food was needed for the men to live.

Captain Smith helped to plant a garden at the fort.

Captain Smith traded with the Woodland people.
He gave them glass beads, copper, and iron.
The Woodland people gave the settlers corn, meat, and furs.
The food they traded helped the men to live.
But some died from sickness.
Because Captain Smith was a wise leader, more men lived.

Captain Smith traded copper pots for food.

What did Captain Smith trade with the Woodland people?

Captain John Smith

Captain John Smith loved to
explore places far away.
He was a short man with red hair.
Captain Smith was a good leader
and a skilled soldier.
While hunting for deer one day,
he was taken by the Indians.
Chief Powhatan did not want
John Smith to live.
But the chief's daughter begged
for the captain's life to be saved.
Captain Smith made friends
with the Woodland people.
He learned their way of life.
He learned to talk with them.
God used John Smith to make
Jamestown a better settlement.

Captain John Smith

Living in the Woods

The Woodland people lived in America long
before men came from England.
Each Woodland family worked together.
Their homes were made from trees.
They made clothes from deer hides.
The men were hunters and fishers.
The women made mats, pots, and baskets.

Boys practiced running and shooting bows and arrows.

Girls pulled weeds in the gardens and found sticks for the fire.

The family used the **resources** from the woods for food and to make homes and clothes. Resources are things we find around us to use.

An Indian Princess

Pocahontas was the daughter of Chief Powhatan.

She was an Indian princess.

But Pocahontas had to work like other girls.

She was a friend to the settlers in Jamestown.

Once Chief Powhatan took some men and guns.

Then a ship's captain took Pocahontas.

The captain wanted Chief Powhatan to return his men and his guns for Pocahontas.

The chief took three months to return them.

Chief Powhatan let Pocahontas live with the English.

Pocahontas took food to the hungry men in Jamestown.

Pocahontas learned the English ways.
A pastor taught her about God.
She trusted in the true God.
Pocahontas loved a Christian man
from Jamestown.
John Rolfe and Pocahontas were married.
He took Pocahontas to visit England.
There the Indian princess met the
queen of England.

John Rolfe and Pocahontas
were married in Jamestown.

Whom did Pocahontas trust
in to become a Christian?

The Settlement Grows

The Jamestown settlers and Woodland people had peace after Pocahontas and John Rolfe were married.

The settlement changed as women came to live in Jamestown.

Families were started, and children were born. Families working together made the settlement a better place to live.

Families worked together in Jamestown.

Servants came to Jamestown with no money. After working seven years, they became free men.

More people came to Virginia. They made laws themselves. They formed a new government. Jamestown was the first lasting English settlement.

The servant stacked wood.

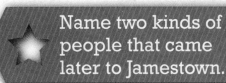

Name two kinds of people that came later to Jamestown.

Activity

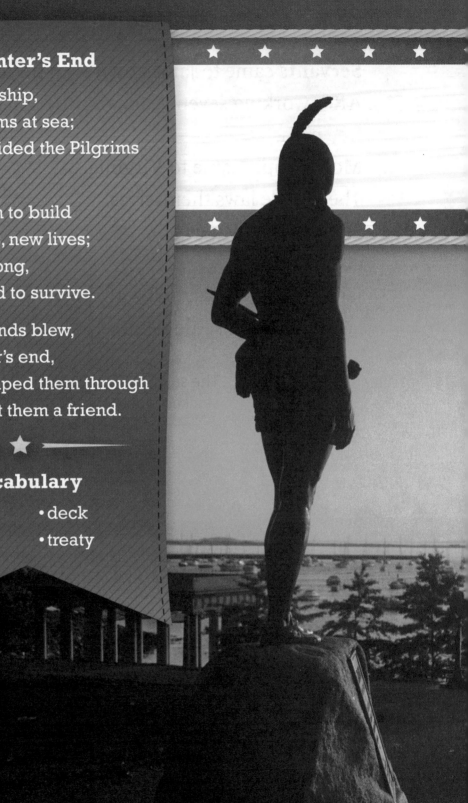

Winter's End

A crowded ship,
Rough storms at sea;
Yet God guided the Pilgrims
Faithfully.

They began to build
New homes, new lives;
All winter long,
They prayed to survive.

The cold winds blew,
Yet at winter's end,
God had helped them through
And brought them a friend.

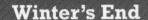

Vocabulary

- beam
- deck
- crew
- treaty

Plymouth

The Pilgrims in England

Some men from England sailed to the New World to find riches.

Other people from England went to find a place to worship God.

The king of England said that everyone must worship in the Church of England.

But the Pilgrims wanted to worship God in their own church.

They believed the Church of England was wrong.

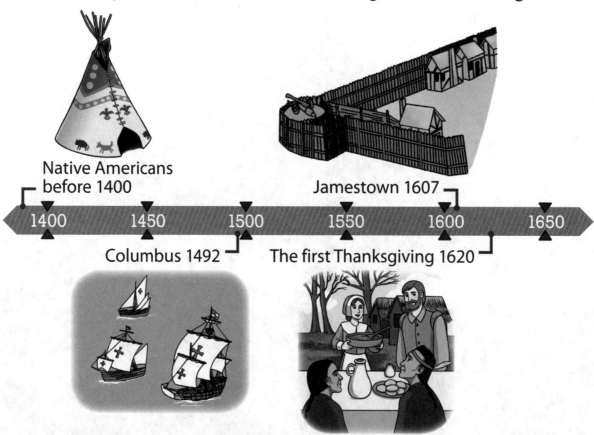

Native Americans before 1400

Jamestown 1607

| 1400 | 1450 | 1500 | 1550 | 1600 | 1650 |

Columbus 1492

The first Thanksgiving 1620

The Pilgrims decided to go to America.
There they could worship the way God
wanted them to.
There they could teach their children
to love God and obey the Bible.

The Pilgrims were
not happy in the
Church of England.

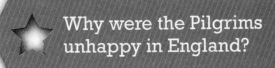

Why were the Pilgrims
unhappy in England?

The Pilgrims on the *Mayflower*

The Pilgrims planned to go to Virginia.
Virginia is part of America.
They hired a **crew** with a ship named
the *Mayflower*.
A crew is the men that work on a ship.
The crew sailed the *Mayflower* across the ocean.

The crew is getting the *Mayflower* ready to sail.

The Pilgrims left England for Virginia.

The Pilgrims lived on the middle **deck**
of the *Mayflower*.
A deck is a floor of a ship.
The Pilgrims stayed in the small, dark area
for many days.
Even the children ate, slept, and played there.

The *Mayflower*

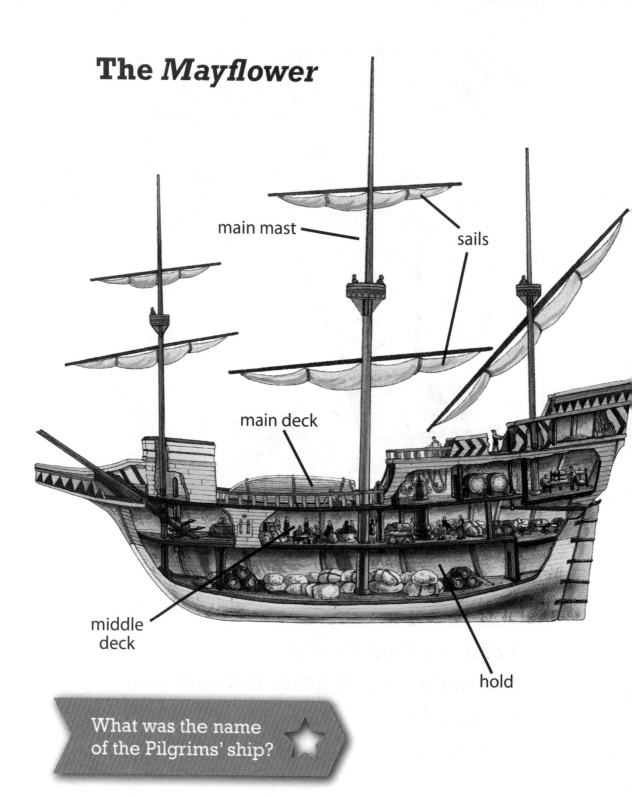

main mast

sails

main deck

middle deck

hold

What was the name of the Pilgrims' ship?

The Pilgrims' Voyage

The voyage on the *Mayflower* was not easy.
But God watched over the Pilgrims.
During a storm a **beam** on the ship cracked.
A beam is a log that holds the deck up.
A Pilgrim had packed a large iron screw.
The crew used the screw to fix the beam.
God knows all things.
He knew the Pilgrims would need that screw.

The *Mayflower* sailed safely through the storm.

Storms had blown the *Mayflower* north,
near Plymouth.
The laws for the Virginia settlement
would not work there.
Now the Pilgrims needed to make new laws.
The laws were called the Mayflower Compact.
The laws in the Mayflower Compact honored
both God and the king of England.

The Mayflower Compact stated that the
Pilgrims would tell others about God.

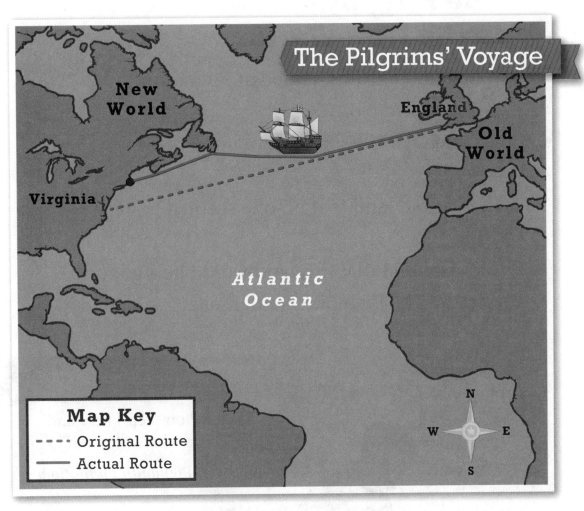

The Pilgrims' Voyage

New World

England

Old World

Virginia

Atlantic Ocean

Map Key
- - - - Original Route
—— Actual Route

N
W
E
S

The dot (•) shows where Plymouth is.

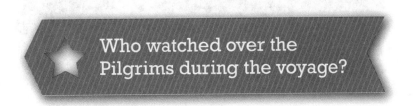

Who watched over the Pilgrims during the voyage?

The Pilgrims in the New World

When the Pilgrims landed at Plymouth, they thanked God.
The men left the ship to look for a place to settle.
They found land that no one seemed to be using.
They decided that this land would be a good place for the Plymouth settlement.

William Bradford

"They fell on their knees and blessed the God of heaven."

Of Plymouth Plantation

The men built houses on the new land.
The women and children stayed on the ship
until their homes were ready.
Some of the crew and the Pilgrims became sick.
The Pilgrims showed God's love.
They cared for each other and the crew.
After many weeks of building houses and a fort,
the Pilgrims moved to the land.

The Pilgrim woman showed God's love to the sick man.

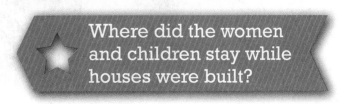

Where did the women
and children stay while
houses were built?

The Pilgrims and the Woodland People

The winter was hard for the Pilgrims.
They had little food, and many died.
One day a Woodland man visited
the settlement.
His name was Samoset.
The Pilgrims were surprised
when he spoke English.
He promised to bring his chief and
his friend Squanto to meet them.

Samoset spoke
to the Pilgrims
in English.

Soon the Pilgrims met the chief and Squanto.
Squanto spoke English too.
He also knew the English ways.
The Pilgrims trusted the Woodland people.
They made a peace **treaty**.
The treaty was a promise to live in peace.
The Woodland people and the Pilgrims lived
in peace for many years.

God blessed the Pilgrims with peaceful friends.

Squanto lived with the Pilgrims in Plymouth.
He taught the Pilgrims how to hunt and fish.
He showed them how to plant corn, beans,
and squash in a hill of dirt.
He taught them to bury a fish with the seeds
to help the plants grow.
Squanto became a friend to the Pilgrims.

Squanto showed the Pilgrims how to plant corn.

Who helped the Pilgrims
learn the ways of the
Woodland people?

Squanto

Squanto was born into a Woodland tribe. He loved his family and the people in his tribe. He ran through the woods with the other boys. And he helped gather shellfish from the waters.

One day, a sea captain kidnapped Squanto. The captain sold Squanto as a slave in Europe. The man who bought Squanto told him about Jesus. Later God allowed Squanto to return home. But his family and tribe had all died. The Pilgrims settled where Squanto had lived. They became his friends. God knew the Pilgrims would need Squanto to help them learn how to live in the New World. God knows all things. He does all things well.

The First Thanksgiving

God blessed the Pilgrims with a new land.
God sent Squanto to teach them.
At harvest time in the fall, there was plenty
of food.
Because the Pilgrims were thankful, they held
a harvest celebration.
The harvest celebration was the first
Thanksgiving.

Philippians 4:19

God shall supply all
your need.

Then and Now

Comparing a Thanksgiving Celebration

Then			
Now			

How was the first Thanksgiving celebration different from a Thanksgiving holiday today?

Activity

In Days of Long Ago

I wonder what the world was like
In days of long ago;
Did people ever phone each other
Just to say hello?

I wonder if they ate hot dogs
Or sat and watched TV?
I wonder if they laughed and loved
The same as you and me?

Vocabulary

- change
- communicate
- future
- past
- present

Today and Long Ago

Change

Things **change** over time.

To change is to become different.

Long ago God told people to fill the earth and care for it.

As people do this, things change.

Your community is different now than it was in the **past**.

The past is the time before now.

The way your community looks now is called the **present**.

This is the way one community's store looked in the past.

Learning About the Past

Ask older people about the past.

Read books about the past.

Look at things and pictures from the past.

What is the past?

Sharing Thoughts

The way we **communicate** has changed over time.
To communicate is to share your thoughts.

1865   1885   1905   1925

We communicate faster and easier today.

1925   1945   1965   1985

What does the word *communicate* mean?

Around Your House

Tools have also changed.
Tools help people get work done.

Used to keep food cold

Used to cook food

Used to clean clothes

Used to make clothes

What did people use
to get work done?

The Future

The **future** is the time that is to come.
Things will keep changing in the future.
Things may change, but we will still work,
share thoughts, and help each other.
God wants us to love and obey Him
and show love to others.
His love will never change.
In the future God will give His people
a perfect world to live in.
That world will never end.

One of the first cars

A car we might
see today

What will cars be
like in the future?

Activity

171

Resource Treasury

Geogloss   A geogloss shows landforms, streams, and bodies of water.   174

Atlas   Maps in an atlas show land and water.   176

   Continents and Oceans   176

   The United States of America   178

Picture Glossary   A picture glossary has pictures and meanings of words.   180

Geogloss

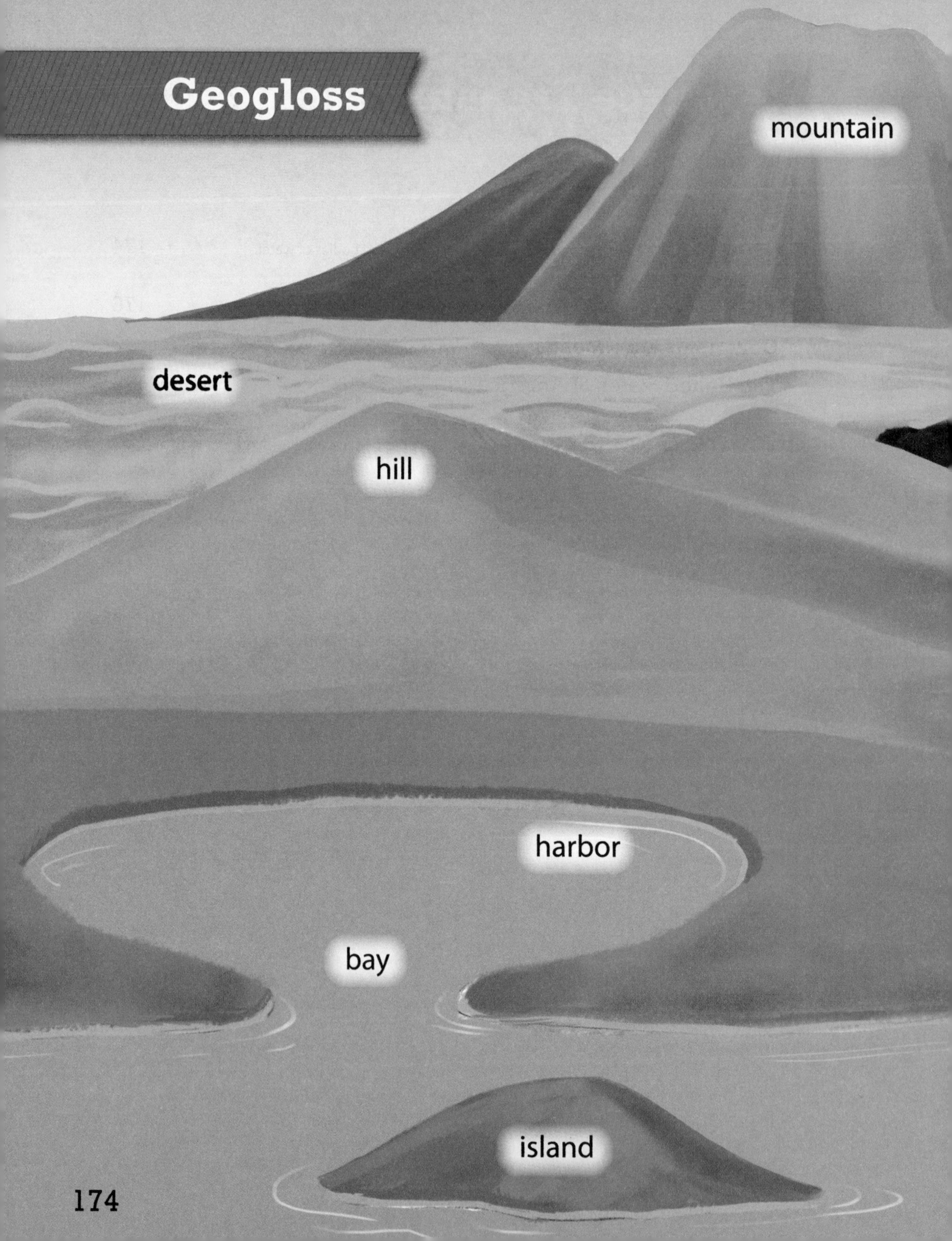

mountain

desert

hill

harbor

bay

island

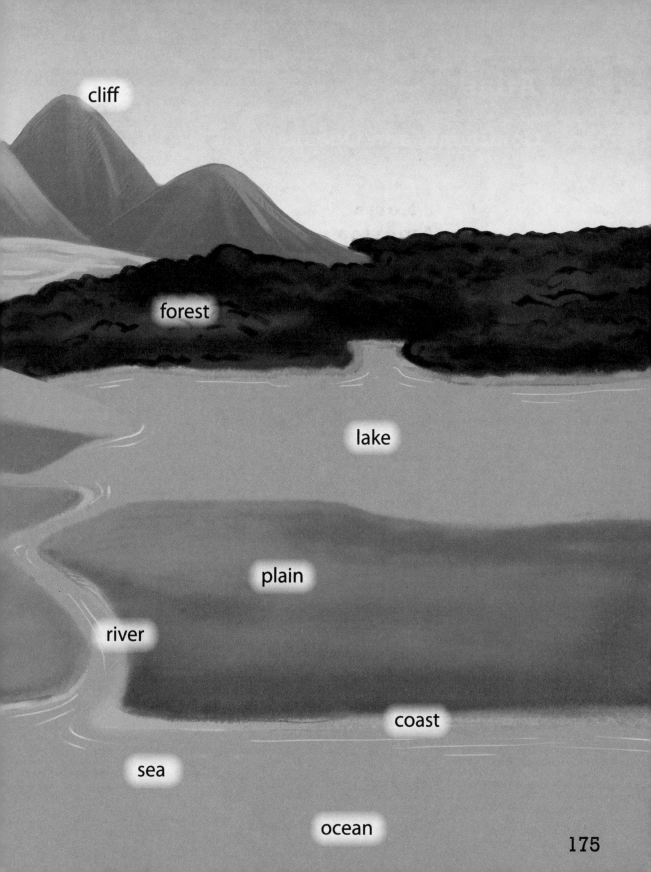

cliff

forest

lake

plain

river

coast

sea

ocean

175

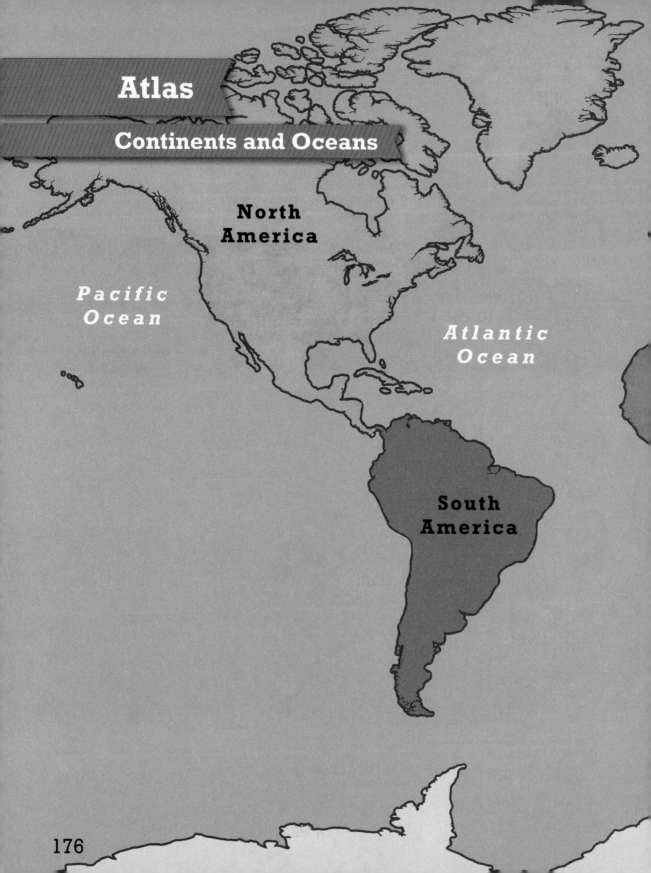

North
America

*Pacific
Ocean*

*Atlantic
Ocean*

South
America

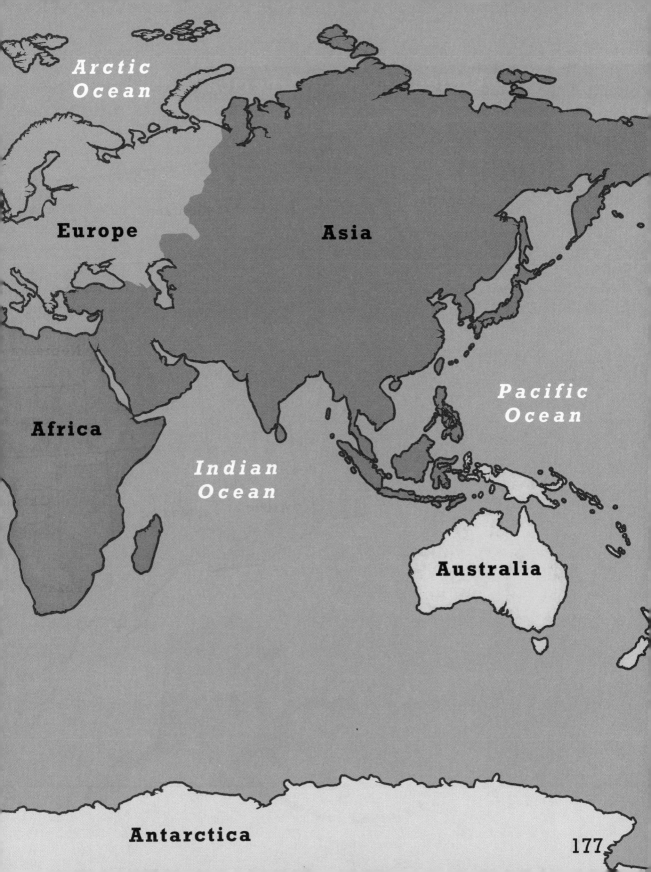

Arctic
Ocean

Europe

Asia

Africa

Indian
Ocean

Pacific
Ocean

Australia

Antarctica

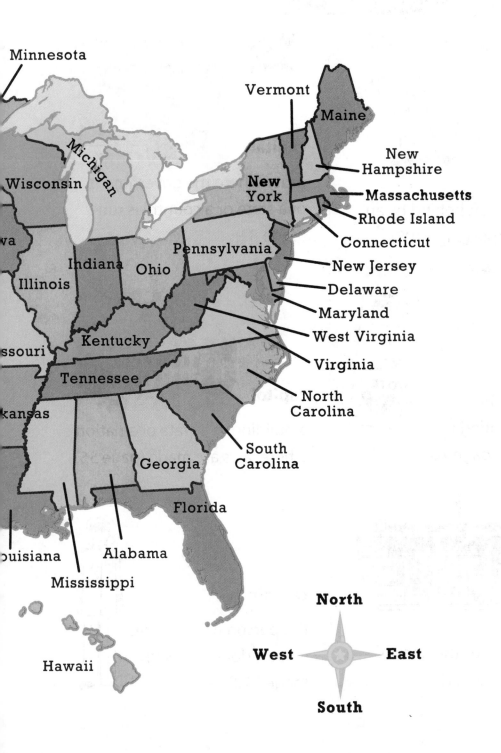

Minnesota

Vermont

Maine

Michigan

New
Hampshire

Wisconsin

New
York

Massachusetts

Rhode Island

Connecticut

Pennsylvania

New Jersey

va

Indiana

Ohio

Delaware

Illinois

Maryland

West Virginia

ssouri

Kentucky

Virginia

Tennessee

North
Carolina

kansas

South
Carolina

Georgia

uisiana

Alabama

Florida

Mississippi

Hawaii

North

West

East

South

179

Picture Glossary

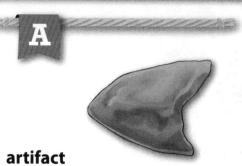

artifact

something left behind by an earlier people (page 108)

ballot

a list of all the people wanting to be elected (page 78)

beam

a log that holds the deck of a ship up (page 151)

capital

a city where the government of a state or a country is run (page 82)

capitol

a building in a state or a nation where laws are made (page 55)

captain

the person who decides what is done on a ship (page 112)

celebrate

to honor someone or something in a special way (page 87)

change

to become different (page 164)

chief

a leader of a tribe (page 130)

citizen

someone who is a member of a country (page 77)

communicate

the sharing of thoughts (page 166)

community

people living or working together (page 36)

continent

one of seven big pieces of land on the earth (page 16)

crew

a group of men that work on a ship (page 148)

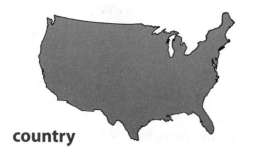

country

a land with its own people and laws (page 52)

culture

a way of life (page 100)

court

a place where judges use laws to settle problems (page 55)

D

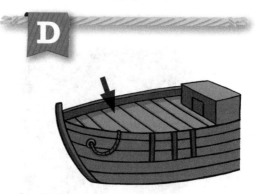

deck

a floor of a ship (page 149)

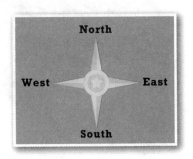

directions

point you to places (page 18)

E

election

when people choose or vote for new leaders (page 78)

explore

to find out about a new place (page 113)

F

family

a father and a mother and their children (page 24)

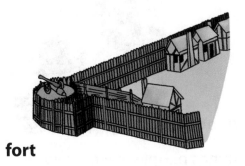

fort

a place that is safe (page 132)

future

the time that is yet to come (page 170)

globe

a ball-shaped object that shows the continents and oceans of the world (page 19)

goods

things people make, grow, or sell (page 37)

government

all the workers that serve the people of a city, state, or country (page 45)

governor

the leader of a state (page 54)

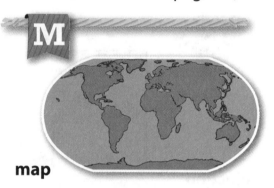

map

a drawing that shows where places are (page 15)

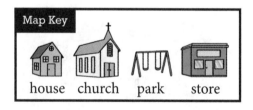

Map Key

house   church   park   store

map key

a box near a map that shows what the pictures mean (page 48)

mayor

the leader of a city (page 44)

motto

an important saying (page 72)

memorial

something that helps you
remember people or times
from the past (page 88)

native

a person born in
a certain place (page 99)

monument

something that stands for a
person in the past (page 86)

needs

things you must have to live
(page 32)

O

ocean

a big body of water; the blue places on a map (page 17)

P

past

the time before now (page 164)

pledge

a promise (page 70)

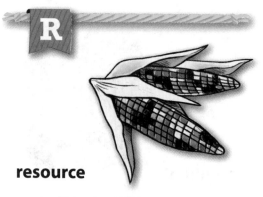

present

the time that is happening now (page 164)

president

the leader of a country (page 58)

R

resource

something you find around you to use (page 139)

right

something you are free to do
(page 77)

role

the special part each family
member plays (page 26)

rule

a statement that tells what may
or may not be done (page 30)

S

sailor

a member of a ship's
crew (page 113)

Savior

Jesus, the One Who
saves people from
their sin (page 13)

servant

a person who works for others
(page 143)

service

doing something to help people (page 38)

state

a part of a country (page 52)

settlement

a group of people living in a new place (page 132)

symbol

something that stands for something else (page 62)

soldier

a person who fights in a war or serves in an army (page 88)

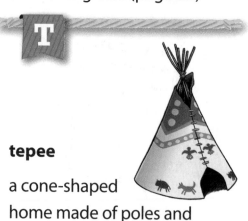

tepee

a cone-shaped home made of poles and buffalo hides (page 103)

totem pole

a tall pole carved with pictures of people and animals (page 107)

treaty

a promise people agree to keep (page 157)

tribe

a group of related people who live in one place and share a common culture (page 100)

veteran

a person who has served in the armed forces (page 89)

vote

to choose (page 78)

voyage

a long trip to a faraway place (page 116)

wants

things you would like to have
(page 33)

Index

A

Adam, 11–12, 14, 24–25
Alabama, 56
Alaska, 64, 107
American flag, 70, 86
American Red Cross, 57
"America the Beautiful,"
 74–75
Arizona, 59
armed forces, 89
artifact, 108–109
Asia, 17, 21, 113–117,
 121

B

bald eagle, 72
ballot, 78
Barton, Clara, 57
beam, 151
Bradford, William, 154
buffalo, 102–103

C

California, 61
Canada, 69
canoe, 106–107
capital, 80–83, 95
capitol, 55, 83, 94–95
captain, 112, 118
Carver, George
 Washington, 56–57
celebrate, 87, 93
change, 164
chief, 130–131, 137, 140,
 156–157
China, 21
citizen, 77–79
city, 44–45, 49
Columbus, Christopher,
 112–121, 123, 126, 146
Columbus Day, 123
communicate, 166–167

community, 34–46, 48–
49, 52, 164
  helpers, 38–39, 42–43
  leaders, 44–45, 49
  places, 40–41
compare and contrast
chart, 47, 161
Constitution, 76, 83
continent, 16, 19, 21, 115
country, 52, 58, 63, 68–
70, 72–73, 76–77, 79,
88–89, 93
court, 55
Creation, 8–11
crew, 148, 155
culture, 20, 100–101

D
deck, 149
directions, 18
dog-sled race, 64
duty, 77

E
election, 78–79
England, 92–93, 127–
128, 138, 141, 146–147,
149, 152
Europe, 17, 21, 113, 159
Eve, 11–12, 14, 24–25
explore, 113, 115, 121,
137

F
Fall, the, 12
family, 22–33, 36, 41–42,
49, 103, 138–139, 142
flag, 53, 70–71, 86
Flag Day, 70
Flood, the, 98
fort, 132–135, 155
Fourth of July, 92–93
Franklin, Benjamin, 46
freedom, 62, 92–93
future, 170

G

globe, 19, 68
Golden Gate Bridge, 61
goods, 37
government, 45, 54, 82, 143
governor, 54
Grand Canyon, 59
Great Lakes, 60–61

H

harvest, 160
holiday, 161
Hopi, 105

I

Independence Day, 92–93

J

Jamestown, 124–125, 129, 132–134, 137, 140–143, 146
judge, 55, 76

K

Kennedy, John, Jr., 85
Kiowa, 102–103

L

Land of the Free, 68
lawmakers, 76, 83
laws, 44, 52, 54–55, 68, 76–77, 83, 143
Liberty Bell, 62
Lincoln, Abraham, 90–91
Lincoln Memorial, 90–91, 94

M

map, 15–19, 114–115, 126
    America's Neighbors, 69
    Community Map, 48
    Jamestown, 129
    Jamestown Fort, 133

map (continued)
  Landmarks in Washington, DC, 94–95
  Native Americans, 100–101
  North America, 18
  Old World and New World, 127
  Pilgrims' Voyage, 153
  Route to Asia, 113
  World, 15
map key, 48
Maryland, 53, 57
Mayflower, 148–152
Mayflower Compact, 152
mayor, 44, 49
memorial, 88–91, 94
Mexico, 69
Michigan, 60
money, 33, 116–117

Montana, 52
monument, 80, 86, 94–95
motto, 72–73
Mount Rushmore, 58

N
native, 99
Native Americans, 97–109, 127, 130, 146
needs, 32–33, 134
New World, 126–127, 146, 154, 159
New York, 63
Niña, 118
North America, 16–18, 98–99, 102, 115
Northwest Coast, 106

O
Obama, Sasha, 85
ocean, 17, 19

P

parade, 49, 89, 92–93

past, 164–165

Pennsylvania, 62

Percy, George, 133

pictograph, 43

Pilgrims, 146–161

Pinta, 118

plains, 100, 102

pledge, 70–71

Pledge of Allegiance, 71

Plymouth, 152–154, 158

Pocahontas, 140–142

Poems

"Dreams and Plans," 110

"Fireworks," 66

"In Days of Long Ago," 162

"My Community," 34

"My God Knows," 6

"No Place Like Home," 50

"Song of Our Homeland," 96

"Star City," 80

"To a Wild New Shore," 124

"Together," 22

"Winter's End," 144

Powhatan, 130–131, 137, 140

present, 164

president, 58, 76, 84–85, 87, 90–91

Presidents' Day, 87

princess, 140

R

recycle, 43

resource, 139

right, 77

role, 26

Rolfe, John, 141–142
Roosevelt, Ted, Jr., 85
rule, 30–31

S
sailor, 113, 116, 118–120
salvation, 13
Samoset, 156
Santa María, 118
Savior, 12–13, 21
scatter, 98
servant, 143
service, 38–39, 41–43
settlement, 132, 134, 137,
  142–143, 152, 154, 156
ship, 112–113, 116, 118–
  119, 122, 128–130
sin, 12–13
Smith, Captain John,
  134–137
soldier, 88
South Dakota, 58

Southwest, 104–105
spirit, 101
Squanto, 156–160
"Star-Spangled Banner,"
  73
state, 52–65, 68, 70
Statue of Liberty, 63
symbol, 62, 70, 72

T
Taylor, Hudson, 21
tepee, 103, 108
Thanksgiving, 146,
  160–161
timeline, 33, 166–167
Tlingit, 107
tool, 168–169
totem pole, 107
trade, 136
treaty, 157
tribe, 100–102, 105, 107,
  130–131

U

United States of America, 52, 68, 70–72, 76–77, 79, 82–83, 87

V

veteran, 89

Veterans Day, 89

Virginia, 128–129, 143, 148–149, 152–153

vote, 78–79

voyage, 116, 119–121

W

wants, 33, 134

Washington, DC, 82–84, 86, 92, 94–95

Washington, George, 86–87

Washington Monument, 86–87, 93–94

White House, 76, 84–85, 94

Woodland people, 130–131, 136–139, 142, 156–159

world, 8–9, 11–12, 14–17, 19–20

World War II Memorial, 88–89, 94

Photograph Credits

The following agencies and individuals have furnished materials to meet the photographic needs of this textbook. We wish to express our gratitude to them for their important contribution.

Alamy
Michael Asire
Associated Press
Bigstock
BJU Photo Services
Brian Collins
Dreamstime
Fotolia

Getty Images
iStockphoto
Brian Jones
Library of Congress
Preservation Virginia
SuperStock
Thinkstock
Wikimedia Commons

Chapter One

Getty Images/Hemera/Thinkstock 6–7; Jose Luis Pelaez/Photographer's Choice/Getty Images 2 (top); © Fancy Collection/SuperStock 2 (bottom); © Steve Vidler/SuperStock 3 (bottom left); © iStockphoto.com/Shawn Gearhart 3 (right); © iStockphoto.com/Chris Bernard 3 (top); Getty Images/Hemera/Thinkstock 4; © iStockphoto.com/DAMIAN KUZDAK 10 (bottom right); © iStockphoto.com/Eduardo Mariano Rivero 10 (bottom right center); © iStockphoto.com/Johannes Kornelius 10 (top right); Getty Images/iStockphoto/Thinkstock 10 (top right center), 10 (top left), 20 (bottom right); © iStockphoto.com/Angelika Stern 10 (bottom left); Jose Luis Pelaez/Iconica/Getty Images 19 (top); BJU Photo Services 19 (bottom); Getty Images/Jupiter Images/Thinkstock 20 (left); Getty Images/Photos.com/Thinkstock 20 (top right)

Chapter Two

© iStockphoto.com/Skip Odonnell 22–23; Getty Images/Stockbyte/Thinkstock 26; Getty Images/iStockphoto/Thinkstock 32; Getty Images/Comstock Images/Thinkstock 33 (top right); Brian Collins 33 (timeline)

Chapter Three

Justin Kase zfivez/Alamy 34–35; Blend Images/Ariel Skelley/the Agency Collection/Getty Images 36; Getty Images/iStockphoto/Thinkstock 37 (top), 40, 45 (bottom), 47 (top right, bottom right, center right); Getty Images/Comstock Images/Thinkstock 37 (bottom), 41 (bottom left); Getty Images/Stockbyte/Thinkstock 38 (left); Getty Images/Comstock Images/Thinkstock 38 (top right); © Tyler Olson/Dreamstime.com 38 (bottom right); Brian Jones 41 (top left); Getty Images/Creatas RF/Thinkstock 41 (right); Getty Images/Fuse 42; Getty Images/Digital Vision/Thinkstock 44; © iStockphoto.com/mathieukor 45 (top); Wikimedia Commons/Public Domain 47 (left), 49 (top); © zsollere - Fotolia.com 47 (center left); Library of Congress 47 (bottom left); BJU Photo Services 49 (bottom)

Chapter Four

Digital Vision/Getty Images 50–51; Getty Images/iStockphoto/Thinkstock 52, 59, 61; ASSOCIATED PRESS 54 (left); AFP/Getty Images 54 (right); © Culver Pictures, Inc./SuperStock 56; Getty Images/Photos.com/Thinkstock 57; Getty Images/Comstock Images/Thinkstock 58; © Henry Georgi/Aurora Open/SuperStock 60; © age fotostock/SuperStock 62; Getty Images/Photodisc/Thinkstock 63; © imagebroker.net/SuperStock 64; Michael Asire 65

Chapter Five

Getty Images/Digital Vision/Thinkstock 66–67; Getty Images/Creatas RF/Thinkstock 68; Getty Images/Comstock Images/Thinkstock 70; © Exactostock/SuperStock 71 © iStockphoto.com/ Jeremiah Barber 72 (left); © iStockphoto.com/Peter Spiro 72 (right); Wikimedia Commons/Public Domain 73; © iStockphoto.com/melhi 74 (top); Getty Images/iStockphoto/Thinkstock 74 (bottom), 75–76; ASSOCIATED PRESS 77; Michael Asire 79

Chapter Six

© Photori Inc./age fotostock/SuperStock 80–81; Cameron Davidson/Photographer's Choice/Getty Images 82; Kmccoy/Wikimedia Commons/GFDL/ CC-BY-SA_-2.0 83; © Spencer Grant/age fotostock/SuperStock 84; SAUL LOEB/Staff/AFP/Getty Images 85 (right); Getty Images/Stringer/Getty Images Entertainment/Getty Images 85 (left); Library of Congress 85 (center); © Michael S. Nolan/age fotostock/SuperStock 86–87; © Wolfgang Kaehler/SuperStock 88–89; Getty Images/ iStockphoto/Thinkstock 90; © iStockphoto.com/ Steve Sucsy 91; rrodrickbeiler/Bigstock.com 92 (top); © Hemis/Alamy 92 (bottom); Michael Asire 93

Chapter Seven

© Paul Thompson Images/Alamy 96–97 (girl); Getty Images/iStockphoto/Thinkstock 96–97 (background); Andreas F. Borchert/Wikimedia Commons/GFDL 1.2/CC-BY-SA-3.0 105 (right); © Wolfgang Kaehler/SuperStock 105 (left); Joel Bennet/Peter Arnold/Getty Images 107 (top left); Getty Images/Hemera/Thinkstock 107 (top right); Michael Asire 107 (bottom); © iStockphoto.com/ Spiritartist 108 (bottom right); Science & Society Picture Library/Contributor/SSPL/Getty Images 108 (top left); Ernest Amoroso, National Museum of the American Indian/Wikimedia Commons/ Public Domain 108 (bottom left); Getty Images/ iStockphoto/Thinkstock 108 (top right), 109 (top right); Wikipedia Loves Art at the Brooklyn Museum/Wikimedia Commons/CC-BY 2.5 109 (center); Phil Schermeister/National Geographic/ Getty Images 109 (bottom left); © Exactostock/

SuperStock 109 (bottom right and top left); © iStockphoto.com/Wellford Tiller 109 (top right)

Chapter Eight

© Mikael Utterstrm/Alamy 110–11; NASA/ Wikimedia Commons/Public Domain 114; © Visions of America/SuperStock 118; U.S. Navy/ Wikimedia Commons/Public Domain 122; BJU Photo Services 123

Chapter Nine

© David Forbert/SuperStock 124–25; Newport News Daily Press/Contributor/McClatchy-Tribune/ Getty Images 128; Courtesy Preservation Virginia 132; Thomas J. Abercrombie/Contributor/National Geographic/Getty Images 137; BJU Photo Services 143

Chapter Ten

© age fotostock/SuperStock 144–45; BJU Photo Services 161

Chapter Eleven

© David Lyons/age fotostock/SuperStock 162–63; Getty Images/Jupiter Images/Thinkstock 164; Getty Images/Hemera/Thinkstock 165 (top), 169 (top); © iStockphoto.com/Cliff Parnell 165 (center); © iStockphoto.com/parema 165 (bottom); Getty Images/Hemera Technologies/Thinkstock 166 (bottom); © iStockphoto.com/Paul Hill 166 (top); © Galló Gusztáv - Fotolia.com 167 (bottom); Getty Images/iStockphoto/Thinkstock 167 (top), 170, 171 (bottom right); Petrified Collection/The Image Bank/Getty Images 168 (top); Hemera Technologies/PhotoObjects.net/Thinkstock 168 (bottom); © iStockphoto.com/Elena Butinova 169 (bottom); © Robert Wilson - Fotolia.com 171 (top); Getty Images/Brand X Pictures/Thinkstock 171 (bottom left)

Picture Glossary

Getty Images/Jupiter Images/Thinkstock 181 (center left); ASSOCIATED PRESS 181 (top right), 184 (top right); Blend Images/Ariel Skelley/the Agency Collection/Getty Images 181 (bottom right); © Steve Vidler/SuperStock 182 (center